OBSESSIONS AND PHOBIAS

BY

SIGMUND FREUD

British Library Cataloguing-in-Publication Data
A catalogue record for this book is available from the
British Library

Contents

Sigmund Freud

Sigismund Schlomo Freud was born on 6th May 1856, in the Moravian town of Příbor, now part of the Czech Republic.

Sigmund was the eldest of eight children to Jewish Galician parents, Jacob and Amalia Freud. After Freud's father lost his business as a result of the Panic of 1857, the family were forced to move to Leipzig and then Vienna to avoid poverty. It was in Vienna that the nine-year-old Sigmund enrolled at the Leopoldstädter Kommunal-Realgymnasium before beginning his medical training at the University of Vienna in 1873, at the age of just 17. He studied a variety of subjects, including philosophy, physiology, and zoology, graduating with an MD in 1881.

The following year, Freud began his medical career in Theodor Meynert's psychiatric clinic at the Vienna General Hospital. He worked there until 1886 when he set up in private practice and began specialising in "nervous disorders". In the same year he married Merth Bernays, with whom he had 6 children between 1887 and 1895.

In the period between 1896 and 1901, Freud isolated himself from his colleagues and began work on developing the basics of his psychoanalytic theory. He published *The Interpretation of Dreams*, in 1899, to a lacklustre reception, but continued to produce works such as *The Psychopathology of Everyday Life* (1901) and *Three Essays on the Theory of Sexuality* (1905). He held a weekly meeting at his home known as the "Wednesday Psychological Society" which eventually developed into the Vienna Psycho-Analytic Society. His ideas gained momentum and by the end of the decade his methods were being used internationally by neurologists and psychiatrists.

Freud made a huge and lasting contribution to the field of psychology with many of his methods still being used in modern psychoanalysis. He inspired much discussion on the wealth of theories he produced and the reactions to his works began a century of great psychological investigation.

In 1930 Freud fled Vienna due to rise of Nazism and resided in England until his death from mouth cancer on 23rd September 1939.

OBSESSIONS AND PHOBIAS
(1895)

I shall begin by challenging two assertions which are often found repeated in regard to the syndromes 'obsessions' and 'phobias'. It must be said, first, that they cannot be included under neurasthenia proper, since the patients afflicted with these symptoms are no more often neurasthenics than not; and secondly, that we are not justified in regarding them as the effect of mental degeneracy, because they are found in persons no more degenerate than the majority of neurotics in general, because they sometimes improve, and sometimes, indeed, we even succeed in curing them.[1]

Obsessions and phobias are separate neuroses, with a special mechanism and aetiology which I have succeeded in demonstrating in a certain number of cases, and which, I hope, will prove similar in a good number of fresh cases.

As regards classification of the subject, I propose in the first place to exclude a group of intense obsessions which are nothing but memories, unaltered images of important events. As an example, I may cite Pascal's obsession: he always thought he saw an abyss on his left hand 'after he had nearly been thrown into the Seine in his coach'. Such obsessions and phobias, which might be called *traumatic*, are allied to the symptoms of hysteria.

Apart from this group we must distinguish: (*a*) true obsessions; (*b*) phobias. The essential difference between them is the following:

Two constituents are found in every obsession: (1) an idea that forces itself upon the patient; (2) an associated emotional state. Now in the group of phobias this emotional state is always one of 'anxiety', while in true obsessions other emotional states, such as doubt, remorse, or anger, may occur just as well as anxiety. I will first attempt to explain the really remarkable psychological mechanism of true obsessions, a mechanism quite different from that of the phobias.

¹ I am very glad to find that the authors of the most recent work on this subject express opinions very similar to mine. Cf. Gélineau (1894), and Hack Tuke (1894).

I

In many true obsessions it is quite plain that the emotional state is the principal thing, since that state persists unchanged while the idea associated with it varies. The girl in Case 1 quoted below, for example, felt remorse in some degree for all sorts of reasons - for having stolen, for having ill-treated her sisters, for having made counterfeit money, etc. People who doubt have many doubts at the same time or in succession. It is the emotional state which remains constant in them; the idea changes. In other cases the idea, too, seems fixated, as in Case 4, of the girl who pursued the servants in the house with an incomprehensible hatred, though constantly changing the individual object.

Now a careful psychological analysis of these cases shows that *the emotional state, as such, is always justified.* The girl in Case 1, who suffered from remorse, had good reasons for it; the women in Case 3 who doubted their powers of resistance to temptation knew very well why. The girl in Case 4, who detested servants, had good reasons for complaining, etc. Only, and it is in these two characteristics that the pathological mark lies, (1) *the emotional state persists indefinitely*, and, (2) the associated idea is *no longer the appropriate original one, related to the aetiology of the obsession, but is one which replaces it, a substitute for it.*

The proof of this is the fact that we can always find in the previous history of the patient, *at the beginning of the obsession*, the original idea that has been replaced. The replaced ideas all have common attributes; they correspond to really distressing experiences in the subject's sexual life which he is striving to forget. He succeeds merely in replacing the incompatible idea by another ill-adapted for being associated with the emotional state, which for its part remains unchanged. It is this *mésalliance* between the emotional state and the associated idea that accounts for the absurdity so characteristic of obsessions.

I will now bring forward my observations and conclude with an attempt at a theoretical explanation.

Case 1. A girl reproached herself for things which she knew were absurd: for having stolen, for having made counterfeit money, for being involved in a conspiracy, etc., according to what she happened to have been reading during the day.

Reinstatement of the replaced idea: She reproached herself with the masturbation she had been practising in secret without being able to renounce it. She was cured by careful surveillance which prevented her from masturbating.

Case 2. A young man, a medical student, suffered from an analogous obsession. He reproached himself for all sorts of immoral acts: for having killed his cousin, for having violated his sister, for having set fire to a house, etc. He got to the point of having to turn round in the street to see whether he had not killed the last passer-by.

Reinstatement: He had been much affected by reading in a quasi-medical book that masturbation, to which he was addicted, destroyed one's morale.

Case 3. Several women complained of an obsessional impulse to throw themselves out of the window, to stab their children with knives, scissors, etc.

Reinstatement: Obsessions based on typical temptations. These were women who, not being at all satisfied in marriage, had to struggle against the desires and voluptuous ideas that constantly troubled them at the sight of other men.

Case 4. A girl who was perfectly sane and very intelligent displayed an uncontrollable hatred against the servants in the house. It had been started in connection with an impertinent servant, and had been transferred from servant to servant, to an extent that made housekeeping impossible. The feeling was a mixture of hate and disgust. She gave as a reason for it that the coarseness of these girls spoilt her idea of love.

Reinstatement: This girl had been an involuntary witness of a love-scene in which her mother had taken part. She had hidden her face, had stopped up her ears, and had done her utmost to forget it, as it disgusted her and would have made it impossible for her to remain with her mother, whom she loved tenderly. She succeeded in her efforts; but her anger at her idea of love having been defiled persisted within her, and this emotional state soon linked itself to the idea of a person who could take her mother's place.

Case 5. A girl had become almost completely isolated on account of an obsessional fear of incontinence of urine. She could no longer leave her room or receive visitors without having urinated a number of times. When she was at home or entirely alone the fear did not trouble her.

Reinstatement: It was an obsession based on temptation or mistrust. She did not mistrust her bladder, but her resistance to erotic impulses. The origin of the obsession shows this clearly. Once, at the theatre, on seeing a man who attracted her, she had felt an erotic desire, accompanied (as spontaneous pollutions in women always are) by a desire to urinate. She was obliged to leave the theatre, and from that moment on she was a prey to the fear of having the same sensation, but the desire to urinate had replaced the erotic one. She was completely cured.

Although the cases I have enumerated show varying degrees of complexity, they have this in common: the original (incompatible) idea has been replaced by another idea, the substituted idea. In the cases which I now append, the original idea has been replaced, but not by another idea; it has been replaced by acts or impulses which originally served as measures of *relief* or as *protective* procedures, and are now grotesquely associated with an emotional state which does not fit them, but which has persisted unchanged, and which has remained as justifiable as it was at its origin.

Case 6. *Obsessional arithmomania.* - A woman found herself obliged to count the boards in the floor, the steps in the stair case, etc. - acts which she performed in a ridiculous state of anxiety.

Reinstatement: She had begun the counting in order to distract her mind from obsessional ideas (of temptation). She had succeeded in doing so, but the impulse to count had replaced the original obsession.

Case 7. *Obsessional brooding and speculating.* - A woman suffered from attacks of this obsession which ceased only when she was ill, and then gave place to hypochondriacal fears. The theme of her worry was always a part or function of her body; for example, respiration: 'Why must I breathe? Suppose I didn't want to breathe?' etc.

Reinstatement: At the very beginning she had suffered from the fear of becoming insane, a hypochondriacal phobia common enough among women who are not satisfied by their husbands, as she was not. *To assure herself that she was not going mad*, that she was still in possession of her mental faculties, she had begun to ask herself questions and concern herself with serious problems. This calmed her at first, but with time the habit of speculation replaced the phobia. For more than fifteen years, periods of fear (pathophobia) and of obsessive speculating had alternated in her.

Case 8. *Folie du doute.* - Several cases showed the typical symptoms of this obsession but were explained very simply. These persons had suffered or were still suffering from various obsessions, and the knowledge that the obsessions had disturbed all their acts and had many times interrupted their train of thought provoked a legitimate doubt about the reliability of their memory. The confidence of each one of us is shaken, and we all of us have to re-read a letter or repeat a calculation if our attention has been distracted several times during the performance of the act. Doubt is a quite logical result when obsessions are present.

Case 9. *Folie du doute (Hesitation).* - The girl in Case 4 had become extremely slow in the performance of all her everyday actions, particularly in her toilet. She took hours to tie her shoe laces or to clean her finger-nails. By way of explanation she said she could not make her toilet while the obsessional ideas were occupying her, nor immediately afterwards. As a result, she had become accustomed to wait a definite length of time after each return of the obsessional idea.

Case 10. *Folie du doute. (Fear of scraps of paper.)* - A young woman had suffered from scruples after having written a letter; at the same time she collected all the pieces of paper she saw. She explained this by confessing to a love which she had formerly refused to admit. As a result of constantly repeating her lover's name, she was seized with a fear that the name might have slipped off the end of her pen, that she might have written it upon some scrap of paper in a pensive moment.[1]

Case 11. *Mysophobia*. - A woman kept washing her hands constantly and touched door-handles only with her elbow.

Reinstatement: It was the case of Lady Macbeth. The washing was symbolic, designed to replace by physical purity the moral purity which she regretted having lost. She tormented herself with remorse for conjugal infidelity, the memory of which she had resolved to banish from her mind. In addition, she used to wash her genitals.

As regards the theory of this process of substitution, I will content myself with answering three questions that arise here.

(1) How can the substitution come about?

It seems to be the expression of a special inherited mental disposition. At any rate, 'similar heredity' is often enough found in obsessional cases, and in hysteria. Thus the patient in Case 2 told me that his father had suffered from similar symptoms. He once introduced me to a first cousin who had obsessions and a *tic convulsif*, and to his sister's daughter, aged eleven, who already gave evidence of obsessions (probably of remorse).

(2) What is the motive for the substitution?

11

I think it may be regarded as an act of defence (*Abwehr*) of the ego against the incompatible idea. Among my patients there are some who remember a deliberate effort to banish the distressing idea or recollection from the field of consciousness. (See Cases 3, 4, 11.) In other cases the expulsion of the incompatible idea is brought about which has left no trace in the patient's memory.

(3) Why does the emotional state that is associated with the obsessional idea persist indefinitely instead of vanishing like other states of our ego?

This question may be answered by reference to the theory of the genesis of hysterical symptoms developed by Breuer and myself.[1] Here I will only remark that, by the very fact of the substitution, the disappearance of the emotional state is rendered impossible.

[1] Cf. the German popular song:

Auf jedes weisse Blatt Papier möcht' ich es schreiben: Dein ist mein Herz und soll es ewig, ewig bleiben.

II

In addition to these two groups of true obsessions there is the class of 'phobias', which must now be considered. I have already mentioned the great difference between obsessions and phobias: that in the latter the emotion is always one of anxiety, fear. I might add that obsessions are varied and more specialized, phobias are more monotonous and typical. But this distinction is not of capital importance.

Among the phobias, also, two groups may be differentiated, according to the nature of the object feared: (1) common phobias, an exaggerated fear of things that everyone detests or fears to some extent : such as night, solitude, death, illnesses, dangers in general, snakes, etc.; (2) contingent phobias, the fear of special conditions that inspire no fear in the normal man; for example, agoraphobia and the other phobias of locomotion. It is interesting to note that these phobias have not the obsessive feature that characterizes true obsessions and the common phobias. The emotional state appears in their instance only under special conditions which the patient carefully avoids.

The mechanism of phobias is entirely different from that of obsessions. Substitution is no longer the predominant feature in the former; psychological analysis reveals no incompatible, replaced idea in them. Nothing is ever found but *the emotional state of anxiety* which, by a kind of selective process, brings up all the ideas adapted to become the subject of a phobia. In the case of agoraphobia, etc., we often find *the recollection of an anxiety attack*; and what the patient actually fears is the occurrence of such an attack under the special conditions in which he believes he cannot escape it.

[1] 'On the Psychical Mechanism of Hysterical Phenomena' (1893*a*)

The anxiety belonging to this emotional state, which underlies all phobias, is not derived from any memory; we may well wonder what the source of this powerful condition of the nervous system can be.

I hope to be able to demonstrate, on another occasion, that there is reason to distinguish a special neurosis, the 'anxiety neurosis', of which the chief symptom is this emotional state. I shall then enumerate its various symptoms and insist on the necessity for differentiating this neurosis from neurasthenia, with which it is now confused. *Phobias*, then, *are part of the anxiety neurosis*, and are almost always accompanied by other symptoms of the same group.

The anxiety neurosis, too, has a sexual origin as far as I can see, but it does not attach itself to ideas taken from sexual life; properly speaking, it has no psychical mechanism. Its specific cause is the accumulation of sexual tension, produced by abstinence or by unconsummated sexual excitation (using the term as a general formula for the effects of, of relative impotence in the husband, of excitation without satisfaction in engaged couples, of enforced abstinence, etc.).

It is under such conditions, extremely frequent in modern society, especially among women, that anxiety neurosis (of which phobias are a psychical manifestation) develops.

In conclusion I may point out that combinations of a phobia and an obsession proper may co-exist, and that indeed this is a very frequent occurrence. We may find that a phobia had developed at the beginning of the disease as a symptom of anxiety neurosis. The idea which constitutes the phobia and which is associated with the state of fear may be replaced by another idea or rather by the *protective procedure* that seemed to relieve the fear. Case 7 (obsessive speculating) presents a neat example of this group: a *phobia along with a true substitutive obsession.*

www.ingramcontent.com/pod-product-compliance
Lightning Source LLC
Chambersburg PA
CBHW021551270326
41930CB00008B/1463